Dear Susan,
  God was so wise when He put you and Pete in our lives! Thank you for your constant love and support.

Choosing the Path of Peace Through the Storms

May our Wonderful God continue to bless you as

"There is something more important to Jesus than our bodily comfort and safety. He cares far more about our spiritual condition. It doesn't necessarily seem more significant to you and me here and now, but it is." Nancy Guthrie

you serve Him.
  As you know, one promise I can make is that God's grace will always be sufficient!

  I love you,
  Cay —
  (2017)

DEDICATION

This is dedicated to my precious husband Jackson!!

Thank you for loving me unconditionally, for deciding to trust God no matter what the outcome, for not being a whiner even though you had lots to whine about.

Way back in the beginning, I remember asking God to help me totally love others the way you did. God answered that prayer. He has given me a deep love for others, a deep concern for their relationship with Jesus and their happiness.

You had an ability to forgive and not hold a grudge or look back. Thank you for that example.

I remember the night you accepted the Lord at a Billy Graham Crusade. You took my hand and said you felt like a new person. You felt like you were wearing a new set of clothes. You felt fresh and free.

You took a hold of your faith and made it real, you made it vibrant and I praise God for His beautiful plan.

Thank you for taking the high road through life.

TABLE OF CONTENTS

Chapter 1	Our History	*Pg. 5*
Chapter 2	Illness That Brought Change to Our Lives	*Pg. 11*
Chapter 3	Accepting Change in the Beginning Is Most Difficult	*Pg. 13*
Chapter 4	Scriptures That Helped Us Deal With the Setbacks	*Pg. 21*
Chapter 5	Heaven	*Pg. 27*
Chapter 6	Personalities Help but Don't Make the Big Difference	*Pg. 29*
Chapter 7	Prayer Made the Difference!	*Pg. 32*
Chapter 8	The Sovereignty of God	*Pg. 36*
Chapter 9	Spritzing God's Grace	*Pg. 39*
Chapter 10	Having a Hunger and Thirst for God's Word	*Pg. 42*
Chapter 11	The Enemy Satan!!	*Pg. 45*
Chapter 12	The Peace That Goes Beyond All Understanding	*Pg. 47*
Chapter 13	There Is No Doubt That God Could Have Healed Jack	*Pg. 51*
Chapter 14	Dream, Struggle, Prize	*Pg. 53*
Chapter 15	I Choose Grandpa	*Pg. 55*
Chapter 16	Faithful Family and Friends Are a Gift	*Pg. 56*
Chapter 17	We Each Show Our Love in Different Ways	*Pg. 59*
Chapter 18	Our Life Is a Tapestry	*Pg. 61*
Chapter 19	Leaving the World and Going Home	*Pg. 63*
Chapter 20	I Am Claiming My Peace and Joy	*Pg. 66*

Preface

The purpose of the words put on these pages is to glorify God for all He has done and to help others who are going through difficult times. We believe every one of us will go through difficult times at one time or another. We see ourselves as common as each of you. Actually, we are honored that God chose us as His children. He loved us enough to be patient with us. He allowed difficult times to chisel away at the rough edges. We learned the hard way as most of us do. As we learned lessons and rejoiced we often asked God how He wanted to use the times we were going through. We didn't want them to be wasted. More than once I had a strong sense from God that I would eventually put some of these lessons on paper.

This is a humble effort to relay to you some of what God taught my husband and me in the last 15 to 20 years. If it can lighten your load or encourage you in any way, it will be worth the effort.

Chapter 1

Our History

"I'm concerned that you girls are going to overdo it when I die. You and Cherrie make it sound like I have been so wonderful. Don't ever forget that I have been no more than a woman of God seeking to honor God with my life. That doesn't mean I haven't made many mistakes. Just don't make it sound like I have been perfect because that is not true." Adina Hofer (my mom)

My Family

This gives you a little idea of the kind of upbringing I had. My parents really were wonderful. The things they did right were centered on honoring God with their lives. They set a wonderful example of being in God's Word daily as a family and privately. We prayed as a family and they prayed on their knees nightly. They admitted when they made mistakes and as a family we were pretty clear with each other on how we felt about most issues. They were not afraid to clear things up with others when there were hurt feelings. My sister Cherrie and I talk often about how blessed we are. I listened in on my mother and her sisters as they discussed doctrine, bad attitudes, and obeying God. They had been covered with prayer by a mom who basically raised 12 children on her own during the Depression. She and my grandpa (until he died at a young age) were totally committed to Jesus and prayed for their family with great passion. It seems to me that God answered their prayers many times over. What a reminder that even though we die, our prayers live on with God answering them for years to come.

My father also came from a Christian home. My grandpa Hofer was one of the most Christ-like men I have known. They too modeled that major disappointments don't stop you from honoring God, loving Him and trusting Him for the future.

Jack's Family

Jack's parents loved him. They were very devoted to their sons, their jobs and their community and were respected. Even though they were churchgoers, they were not as vocal about their faith.

As a child Jack practiced piano for two hours a day. When he got older some of that time was replaced with practice on the trumpet. I only say this to point out that he grew up being disciplined to commit to what was important to him. He would not have done that on his own. I often heard him tell others that he would not have been where he was musically, if his mother had not insisted that he practice so much. She helped develop that discipline. Jack often told me that we can become professional at most anything if we work hard at it long enough. Jack was excellent on the piano and most instruments. He excelled in high school and college musically. He learned commitment and excellence from his parents.

Our Immediate Family

Jack and I got married in 1964. I worked on my undergraduate and he completed his Masters. Because of the band director-teaching job, we moved to Rawlins, Wyoming. Our two sons were born and dedicated to the Lord in Rawlins. Matt was born in 1966 and Jeff in 1967. In 1968 we moved to Winona, Minnesota where we have been able to spend the rest of our years together. Jack loved being a band director. Not once did he hint that he didn't want to go to work. The bands Jack produced showed his same commitment to excellence. He challenged his students more than would have been expected. He loved the students and they loved him. He loved performing. He loved having his students perform well. He loved the thrill of teaching them and hearing them achieve. He shed tears the day he decided to retire from teaching. And tears were rare in those days. It was a huge decision to retire from what he loved. He retired at age 55 because of a package the state put out to teachers of his age and years of experience.

I taught voice and piano privately along with working a networking business that has enhanced our lives.

Basically, I have been blessed to be home when I wanted to. I was able to spend time with people encouraging them spiritually, musically and in their business.

As was the case in my upbringing, family time in God's Word and praying together has been a commitment to us. Jack was good at being in charge. Our sons would tell you that we had more family conferences than many other families put together. Far too often, our family devotions turned into family conferences. The boys used to say, "Can we just have devotions and not a family conference?"

I will share with you one incident that gives you an idea of how we lived. One Sunday when the kids were in high school, we were all over tired and grouchy. We were at each other on the way to church. When we got there we were all smiles like usual. The second we got back into the car the attitudes were back. Jack said we would have a 'family conference' as soon as we got home. We wouldn't eat until we talked things through.

Around the bare table, Jack discussed each of the kids' activities. There was school, working, youth group, hunting, etc. He said something had to go. They were so tired that they had become disrespectful and unkind. Matt, our non-talker, had one tear coming down his cheek as he said, "Dad, I agree totally with what you just said but I have to say something. Please don't take this as a sass because it is not meant to be one. You and Mom are just as bad." It instantly became very quiet. We all knew it was true. We were both responsible for many musical groups coming up for the Christmas season in addition to the Bible studies we were leading and other normal responsibilities. After a couple minutes to gain his composure, Jack said, "You're right. We will each pray about this for one week. We will ask God to show us what to give up and then we will discuss it next Sunday. We will not discuss it until then. At that time we will tell the other what is going to change in each of our lives." We agreed.

I don't remember what Matt and Jeff gave up but they did give things up. Jack and I did not discuss this all week. One week later, we each sincerely felt led to give up a big responsibility in church, Jack as organist and I as choir director. I distinctly remember the other three being extremely surprised when each of us told how we had been led by the Lord that week. We were all amazed that God would tell us to give up a ministry. The boys' exact words were, "Oh, we didn't mean you had to do that. We know how much that means to you." Jack and I were totally at peace and carried through with how God had spoken to us. There are stories that reinforce that God indeed had led us and we were doing the right thing. I love those confirmations.

Jack was also good at admitting when he had a bad attitude and would ask us to pray for him. Even though I grew up with that, he found it easier to do that as an adult than I did. I'm there now but it didn't come as easily for me. Even though I grew up being loved I grew up with low self-esteem. That was probably due to being very overweight. I was 30 years old when I thanked God for how I was made and accepted myself as I was. Even though Jack also grew up overweight, it never affected his self-esteem.

Praying together allowed us to know each other's hearts.

Jack was the love of my life. We learned so much from each other and appreciated the balance God brought into our relationship by blending our two backgrounds.

We each found it so necessary to spend time with Jesus individually and together. Jack spent significant time with the Lord each day before he went to work. I too always found morning was the best time for me to be alone with Jesus. The evening was our time to pray together. Praying together allowed us to know each other's hearts. It has always been the first bit of advice we gave to couples wanting to grow stronger in their relationship.

Chapter 2

Illness That Brought Change To Our Lives

The only one who likes change is a wet baby.
Mark Twain

This is not meant to be a book on serious back pain, diabetes, vascular problems, broken feet, lost toes, or Parkinson's. I will briefly comment on these stresses simply because these are the reasons for our struggles.

Jack inherited diabetes from his mom. He was not good at taking care of his body. He ate too much, did not work out, did not seem to need much sleep, and thrived on a busy life. He would be the first to admit that the severity of the problems associated with diabetes were there because he was negligent in the areas mentioned above. Those issues wore on him. He felt responsible. Because of the neuropathy, his balance became bad, feet hurt, he lived in pain and things started slowing down. He broke a foot falling out of an elevator that stopped 3 feet above the floor. He ran to break the fall but since he didn't have feeling, he didn't know he had broken his foot. We actually went on a mission trip with his broken foot in total ignorance of what we were doing to the future of his feet.

Cellulitis was a common enemy causing emergency room trips and hospital stays more often than I want to recount. Jack got delirious at a temperature of 102. We had many interesting trips to our local hospital.

Parkinson's set in around 2004. It set us up for a whole list of new things to learn. Everything went very slowly allowing us to process and feel sorry for ourselves.

Jack did not handle medications well. Because of that he lived with a good deal of pain.

I tell you even this much of his physical problems to emphasize that our journey took place over about 15 years. There were multiple surgeries for toes lost, three vascular surgeries, severe infections, procedures for back pain and finally the deep brain stimulator put in his head to stop the tremors. Many of these were successful, but each took its toll. Each was a process in itself preparing us emotionally and physically. At one point, he was in the hospital 15 times in two years.

Chapter 3

Accepting Change in the Beginning...
Is The Most Difficult!

Life's turning points are as sure as the tide.
Just a matter of when, so why not decide
To embrace these transitions as ways to grow?
'Tis folly to ignore what you already know.

Make a vow to adapt to the crises of life.
There's no reason to suffer more stress or strife.
Quite often change becomes a blessing in time
While making you wiser in pursuit of your prime.

No change is impossible, no one is exempt.
You can step out in faith or shrug with contempt.
Life comes in cycles, no two are the same.
To claim nothing's new is a naïve game.

But most things do change, it's a natural law.
You can believe this is truth or stand in awe.
It may be uncomfortable, it may cause pain.
Won't a regretful heart be a greater stain?

With every change, there's an outcome to bear.
So accept the challenge, for life's seldom fair.
Be willing to risk and you're bound to find
More courage and strength from a positive mind.

Ah, life has turning points, they won't disappear.
Rise up to greet them and conquer your fear.
The choice is simple, it's as clear as can be.
Will I master change or will change master me?

Will I Master Change or Will Change Master Me?
By Dick Biggs

 We have often said that the beginning of Jack's physical problems was more difficult than the final years even though the final years were more intense. It's just that in the beginning you don't know what to expect and you don't know how to handle what is thrown in your path.

We had been leading a musical group Jubilee. Our purpose was to glorify Jesus musically, to encourage believers, and to help lead others to a personal relationship with Christ. We were a vocal ensemble of 8–12 people who met every week to rehearse. We gave concerts, did some recording and loved what we were doing. We had become a family and leaned on each other immensely. I directed vocally but Jack was the brains musically and did all the accompanying.

You would think retirement would be the time to really commit to a group like this but unfortunately, it was not working. We had been together for 22 years. We had practiced, given our testimonies, shared our hearts with our audience, and prayed together for years. It became too hard for Jack. The last year was extremely stressful wondering if he was going to make it through the concerts. We could not depend on his strength for the day and if he wasn't there, we couldn't be there either. Actually, we probably could have recorded the accompaniment and traveled with it, but somehow Jack was too much of the real thing to go on without him. When we gave Jubilee up, it was a big deal. Sometime before that, we had given up other musical ministries. Soon after these decisions, he was not able to play the piano for his own satisfaction anymore. It was a huge thing emotionally when he could no longer make those piano keys ring.

Sometime after this he gave up using the computer; then golf had to go, and eventually driving. All of this was over the course of years. Jack is not the only one who has had to give up what he loved the most nor will he be the last one. I only trust that reading this will help those of you who also are giving up what you are good at. While giving up those things he loved was difficult, his sense of loss was not in vain. He slowly learned to find his identity in Christ alone. God opened new doors of ministry and gave us peace.

It is easy to say that what we are in Christ is all that matters; however, when satisfaction and pride coming from using your giftedness and God-given abilities are taken away, there is a new reality to the significance of our identity in Christ. It truly can become life changing to totally comprehend that God sees us as precious and valuable in His sight not because of what we do but because of what He has done for us. Then we see our true identity in Christ. Our pastor has often said, "We don't realize that God is all we need until He is all we have."

When I said the beginning times were the hardest, these are some of the things I was referring to. Physical issues are not only physical, they bring with them mounds of emotional issues to work through. Sometimes, the emotional hurts are worse than the physical ones.

I chose to give up the music ministries. After 30 years of accompanying each other as we did solos, (mine vocal and his instrumental). I just couldn't bring myself to have others accompany me and have him sit and listen. It was not until years into all of this that I even sang for funerals and later other functions. By then we had worked through much of the struggle.

Giving up these things that were so dear to us took a few years. We prayed, we cried, we argued telling each other to let it go. I felt sorry for myself when I gave up the music ministry even though I didn't need to physically. I had to work through my own self-pity problem. It was a process that flared up and then after times in God's Word and prayer would settle down only to flare up

We don't realize that God is all we need until He is all we have.

again and send us back into God's presence. I can't tell you when it was gone. It didn't happen in one particular instant. Slowly God brought healing and we were able to let it go. Once that victory was won, others came more easily. Giving up what we love the most sets the stage for working through hurts and disappointments to come. It, like anything else, becomes easier the more you work on it.

While there were many issues we struggled with, I am struck by the fact that never ever did Jack ask God why. In fact, he would often say, "Why not me?" Never did he complain on and on to people about what he couldn't do. If he mentioned it, it was short-lived and didn't become a downer. The Lord gave Jack a new ministry of showing the world that he could live in peace and joy without all the trimmings that once gave him satisfaction.

Jack struggled with not being able to help our sons with any work around their homes, yard, or business. We have used *Five Love Languages* by Gary Chapman and Ross Campbell as a family and found it to be helpful. We knew helping our sons was a love language for each of them that would encourage them and remind them of our love. I remember Jack shedding tears over the fact that now he could do nothing physical for Matt and Jeff. That was something he was so looking forward to in retirement. Even though they understood and they knew their dad loved them, it was a part of life Jack didn't want to give up.

We are pushers. We will try and push ourselves until it is nearly impossible. We were determined to enjoy life as much as possible, to do as much as we could to seem normal. We went from the big boots to crutches, to a cane, to a walker and then to a wheelchair. Each of those steps was a blow to Jack's pride and dignity. You work through it slowly until it too becomes the norm. It became more work to travel just helping Jack in and out of the car, lifting the wheelchair and getting around wherever we were going. Of course there are places the wheelchair simply does not work. Sometimes we didn't anticipate the situation just as it was. Jack always felt so sorry for me pushing him. I never felt pushing was hard. It was the lifting of the chair and getting him in and out of both the chair and the car that was difficult.

One time a few months before he died, we got caught in a whiteout, full scale snowstorm. It was one of those times we should not have been on the road. We pulled off the highway to stay in a motel. The wind was so fierce I knew I wouldn't get Jack out of the car and into the wheelchair without him falling or possibly the car door would close on us before I got him in the chair. I found a young man and asked him to help. He held the chair and helped get Jack in the motel. We spent two days and two nights there. It was difficult without a handicap room and he did fall two times, but we had learned how to work together to get his body back in the chair. The second day we decided we needed to have a party. The only thing we could think of was to eat food out of the vending machine. I can't say it was the most fun party I've ever had but it served its purpose. We appreciated being off the road and warm.

We have a 1963 Pontiac Lemans convertible, red with white leather interior. It is a beaut!!! This became Jack's pride and joy. We had a Pontiac Lemans hardtop when we got married. He loved to tell our story. He had pictures of us leaving after our wedding in our Pontiac at the time. We would go to car shows, go around looking at others' cars and Jack got to talk his heart out covering every detail of our car. He loved it. I had to pray much to improve my attitude. Going to car shows, looking at and talking cars was not my idea of a fun Saturday. I would worry about what we were going to do if he had to go to the bathroom. What if the bathroom is far away and we can't get there? What if we had to head home and we were parked in a place we couldn't get out of until others moved??? I stewed!!!! By this time Jack was finding it easier to trust the Lord to work things out. I was lagging behind. He would remind me that we had never had a problem in the past. He had peace about going and was looking forward to it. God would take care of it. I must say that although car shows will never be my favorite, after a couple years, God graciously changed my heart. I remember one day walking around thanking God that I was enjoying the day. I actually started enjoying listening to others talk passionately about their cars.

After the DBS (deep brain stimulator) surgery his speech became hard to understand. His voice was also getting weaker. Each year got worse. Finally, it was too hard to get out of the Pontiac so he stayed in the car even at the root beer stand on Cruise Night. Many of his friends came over to encourage him and remind him of how beautiful his car was. Finally, he was ready to let this go too. He said, "It's time to let this go. My friends all come to me. I'm not looking at their cars anymore. I can't talk to them so they can understand me. This isn't right. I'm ready to quit." I felt so sorry for him but was so proud of him and the way he handled it. He gave it up and didn't look back. Even though he held onto the car for a long time, giving it up was easier than giving up the music abilities. With God's grace, Jack had learned the gift of letting go.

CHAPTER 4

SCRIPTURES THAT HELPED US DEAL WITH THE SETBACKS

"Even though the world praises independence, I am not ashamed to say that I am dependent on God's Word to refresh my spirit. The more I am in His Word, the more I am able to hear His voice and live in peace." Coy Herr

When people would ask how we were, we tried to convey without going into a lengthy spiritual routine that we were alright but only because we kept going back to work things out with the Lord. It took us years to get to the place where we almost instantly gave the situation back to Jesus. It was time-consuming, it was emotional and it was work!! But it did work!! Going to the Lord, pouring your heart out to Him, asking Him to speak does work. Jack would say it works for anyone who is willing to ask and seek. We would have told you that we were accustomed to spending precious time with the Lord on a one to one basis, and we were; still, there is something about being needy and deeply desiring to understand God's Word and hear from Him that adds to the depth of that time spent with Him. When I read my personal notes written in my devotional, I am often amazed that I am still working on the same issue much later. Other times I realize I had wrestled with an issue that is now a non-issue. It has always been a reminder that our growth in Christ is an ongoing activity. Only when we get to heaven will we be perfect and have it all together.

The parentheses following scripture reference contains the comments we wrote in the margins of our Bible.

As for God, His way is perfect; the word of the Lord is tried. He is a Shield to me because I trust and take refuge in Him. For who is God but the Lord? And who is a Rock except our God? God is my strong Fortress; He guides the blameless in his way and sets me free. II Samuel 22:31-33 AMP (We find the more we trust Him, the freer we are of discontent and fear.)

When I am afraid, I will trust in You. In God, whose word I praise, in God I trust; I will not be afraid. Psalm 56:3-4 NIV

I trust in God at all times. I pour out my heart before Him; God is a refuge for me. Psalm 62:8 AMP

I lean on, trust in, and am confident in the Lord with all my heart and mind and I do not rely on my own insight or understanding. In all my ways I know, recognize, and acknowledge Him, and He directs and makes straight and plain my paths. I am not wise in my own eyes. Proverbs 3:5-8 AMP (We have come to realize that it makes no sense to try to figure out all the details. Our part is simply to trust Him.)

The fear of man brings a snare, but whoever leans on, trusts in, and puts his confidence in the Lord is safe and set on high. Proverbs 29:25 AMP (Satan sends the fear.

The Lord calms my fears when I trust Him. Faith is the answer to my fears.)

In repentance and rest is my salvation; in quietness and trust is my strength. Isaiah 30:15 NIV

When I feel hurt or brokenhearted God binds up my wounds and cures my pain and sorrow. Great is our Lord and mighty in power; his understanding has no limit. Psalm 147:3 & 5 AMP (Thank You, Lord, for always being there and understanding me.)

I am learning how to be content (satisfied to the point where I am not disturbed or disquieted) in whatever state I am. Philippians 4:11 AMP (Keep teaching me Lord. Thank You for Your patience.)

Weeping may endure for a night, but joy comes in the morning. Psalms 30:5 AMP (I have seen and experienced that joy so many times . . . joy that has come after the weeping.) God has not given us a spirit of fear but of peace and a sound mind. II Timothy 1:7

Do not be anxious about anything, but in everything, by prayer and petition, with thanksgiving, present your request to God. And the peace of God, which transcends all understanding, will guard your hearts and your minds in Christ Jesus. Philippians 4:6-8 AMP (He says we should pray about everything and give praise and thanks to Him. When we do that He promises to give peace beyond all comprehension. That kind of peace will protect us. I need to recognize the things about God that are always true no matter what is happening and how afraid I am. I need to thank Him that He is greater than all my needs. Even when my worst fears come upon me, it is God's love for me that assures me that He will bring me out of the situation.)

"My grace is all you need, for my power is greatest when you are weak." I Corinthians 2:9 GNT (Sometimes we want escape from our weakness, not power in our weakness.)

"Don't panic. I'm with you. There's no need to fear for I am your God. I'll give you strength. I'll help you. I'll hold you steady, keep a firm grip on you." Isaiah 41:10 MSG (Jesus came to live inside of us so we can begin to see life with His eyes, touch with His hands and think like He does. However, He will not force that union on us. It's like trying to rescue someone who is drowning who doesn't want to trust you. Jesus says, "Let me rescue you!".)

Some thoughts from *Jesus Calling* by Sarah Young:

"Whenever you find yourself worrying about the future, repent and return to Me. I will show you the next step forward, and the one after that, and the one after that. Relax and enjoy the journey in my presence, trusting Me to open up the way before you as you go."

"Abundant Life is not necessarily health and wealth; it is living in continual dependence on Me." Anxiety wraps you up in yourself, trapping you in your own thoughts. When you look to me and whisper My Name, you break free and receive My help."

"Come to Me for understanding, since I know you far

better than you know yourself. I comprehend you in all your complexity; no detail of your life is hidden from Me."

These verses and thoughts contain some of the truths that we purposely repeated out loud. We often reminded each other that we needed to rehearse the blessings in our lives, not the disappointments. We verbally repeated truths from God's Word, not what we were feeling that day. There is power in God's Word. Read it, speak it, and claim it!! When we do, the storms in our lives don't destroy us. The way we choose to live our lives is always a choice. We can wallow and complain our way through on our own, or we can turn it over to our Heavenly Father and let Him carry the load. I have said before and I will say many times over that it is very freeing to hand the burden over to Him and let it be His responsibility. Our job is to trust, love and hang on close to our dear Heavenly Father. That is the one condition to living with His peace.

When we hurt and learn to lean on, and trust Him, we experience His grace in a way that we do not experience when everything is going well.

We tried it both ways. The more we trusted, the easier it became. Even though we were not new Christians, it took a while for us to get to the point where we could turn it all over to Him and live in peace. There is a calm, a joy that comes from praising Him for all He has provided.

I believe our greatest growth comes from going through

difficult times. When we hurt and learn to lean on and trust Him, we experience His grace in a way that we do not experience when everything is going well. Honestly, we need the hard times to grow in grace.

CHAPTER 5

HEAVEN

"My home is in heaven, I'm just traveling through this world." Billy Graham

For years we talked about heaven. We never saw it as morbid but as a source of joy and anticipation. We loved music and books about heaven. Randy Alcorn's book *Heaven* touched us greatly.

We came to realize that technically, we have far more treasure in heaven than we do in earth. We also have many family and friends in heaven who were very instrumental in our lives. All of that makes the draw to heaven greater. Now that my honey is there, my desire is even greater.

When one of our former pastors, Pat Clinton, was dying of a brain tumor, Jack wanted to talk to him. Since Jack was hard to hear and understand, he asked me to send an email for him. Jack was a newer Christian when Pat and Colleen came to our church in 1971. In the email he thanked Pat for being very patient with him as a new Christian. Then he said, "I always thought I would be the first one in heaven (of the two of them) and would be greeting you at heaven's gate when you arrived. It looks like you will be greeting me when I arrive." We were still able to drive to Rockford, Illinois for Pat's funeral. The entire day was a spiritual encouragement to us. Pat's theme was "Only one life will soon be past. Only what's done for Christ will last!" Pat saw his death as a graduation to heaven. He was the one who had taught us about the dash. The dash is the time between our birth and our death. How am I using my time here on earth? What am I doing with my dash? I can't tell you how all these thoughts gave us courage for a long time to come. The notes in my journal after that weekend say, "Keep our hearts soft like they are now. Don't let us miss Your still small voice. We need to bathe in Your love and presence." We were so thankful for the many different avenues God uses to keep our eyes on Him.

Back in 1971, I personally remember the first time Pat called on us as our pastor. He put his arms around Jack when he left, gave him a big hug and said, "I love you, brother." The last time our Pastor Rick Iglesias visited Jack before he died, he put his arms around Jack and said, "I love you, Jack." How blessed we are!!!

Chapter 6

Personalities Help but Don't Make the Big Difference

"My grace is all you need. My power works best in weakness."
II Corinthians 12:9

Jesus provides what we need when we need it. Jack was beyond a shadow of a doubt the one who was the life of the party, the talker, the positive thinker, the outgoing look at things half full not half empty person. He was the fun one to be with. That also made him the louder, sometimes overdo it person.

I am without question of a different nature. I analyze, worry, have to have everything in order and am very serious about most things. My personality type is not necessarily what you would call fun to be with. I realize we each have the positive and negative of our personality.

I would say that Jack's personality certainly helped him go through these hard years with a better spirit than I would have. At the same time, I want to point out that what he went through and the way he handled everything went far beyond positive thinking. It was Jack's willingness to give it up to Jesus that made the difference.

Secondly, it was Jack's willingness to claim for himself all that our Heavenly Father offers. And that thought, more than any, I want to make clear in this book. I truly believe that anyone of us, no matter what our personality, can experience peace through our trials. It is a choice. It is easy to say, "I'm just not the positive type" or "I never have found it easy to trust God" or "There has to be a reason" or "This isn't fair" or "I've never been religious" or "I don't know the Bible" or a hundred other reasons why we more than anyone cannot live in peace. God's peace is available to all, period.

While there were many struggles along the way, I started to realize that Jack's response to circumstances was supernatural. I had always been proud of Jack, loved his spirit and the way God made him. He was the love of my life. But . . . he was not perfect. There came a time when I realized as wonderful as he was, his response to life was not normal. It was supernatural.

One day I wrote, "This has to be a miracle. No one can be so patient, kind, grateful, peaceful, non-fault finding, have no self-pity, but totally trust Jesus, as he

There is a tradeoff . . . we give God our disappointment and He gives us peace.

struggles to eat, get dressed, walk or do anything on his own. No one can do all that and never change without God having done a miracle." This was beyond Jack. This is very important for us as a family to have others understand. As much as we loved and adored Jack as our dad and husband, we want everyone to know that he handled what he did in the way he did because of his willingness to give it up to Jesus. I've said this before. He was no more special that you and me. One day, as we observed with concern someone struggling with their plight in life, Jack said, "God doesn't love us any more than He does anyone else. Our life isn't a piece of cake either. We have just chosen to trust Him. They can do the same." There is a tradeoff . . . we give God our disappointments and He gives us peace. God's peace is always offered. He is waiting for our willingness to accept it.

CHAPTER 7

PRAYER MADE THE DIFFERENCE!

"Prayer is the difference between seeing with our physical eyes and seeing with our spiritual eyes." Mark Batterson

We would all agree that prayer makes a difference, that it is powerful and life changing. Still, I think we sometimes live like it doesn't really matter because if we did believe it, we would pray more. Prayer doesn't always mean our desires are going to be answered just as we prayed. It honors God that we are coming to Him, and consulting Him. It heals our hurts, encourages our hearts, it helps us see life through different eyes. I'm sure we learned some lessons that only could be learned through a course in pain and suffering. There is no point in trying to pray away the problem until we learn the lesson He is trying to teach us.

Nancy Guthrie says, "God's discipline is always good for us." Hebrews 12:7-10. "What allows us as God's children to endure it is that while it is painful, we're confident it's purposeful. Never punitive. Never random. Never too harsh. Always out of love. What's the purpose? God's desire is that 'afterward there will be a peaceful harvest of right living for those who are trained in this way'

Hebrews 12:11. God is at work cutting away the dead places and destructive patterns in our lives so we can flourish and grow." I want to clarify that we experienced God changing our hearts. God answered multiple prayers of healing issues both physically and spiritually. God provided encouragement, people, and many other avenues that were beyond any doubt an answer to prayer. We could sense others were praying.

During the time of so many emergency trips and or hospital stays, we started getting embarrassed over how many times we asked for prayer or had our pastor with us at the hospital. Every now and then we decided not to tell anyone, just let them off the hook! We did that more than once. In retrospect, when we looked back, we could see a definite difference in how things went. There would be more anxiety, more mistakes, and longer periods of down time. Every time we were covered by prayer from family and friends, things were on a much more even keel. We felt a distinct difference. After that big revelation, we swallowed our pride and asked for prayer for each crisis.

This is one of the many songs we came to love.

SOMEONE IS PRAYING FOR YOU

When it seems that you prayed
till your strength is all gone,
and your tears fall like raindrops all the day long,
Jesus cares and He knows just how much you can bear.
He'll speak your name to someone in prayer.
Someone is praying for you ...

And when it seems you're all alone
and your heart would break in two,
Remember, someone is praying for you.
Have the clouds round you gathered
in the midst of a storm?
Is your ship tossed and battered?
Are you weary and worn?

Don't lose hope, someone is praying
for you this very day,
and peace be still is already on the way.
Someone is praying for you.
Someone is praying for you.
And when it seems you're all alone,
and your heart would break in two,
Remember, someone is praying for you.

Someone Is Praying For You
by Lanny Wolfe

There is no point in carrying your burden alone. The Lord gives us to each other for many reasons, one of those being to lift each other up to Him in prayer.

We always felt that we were washed in peace as we prayed. Beth Moore in *Breaking Free* says, "The spirit of God released through prayer turns cowards into conquerors, chaos into calm, cries into comfort."

Someone said, "You can do more than pray after you have prayed, but you cannot do more than pray until you have prayed. Prayer is striking the winning blow." In Jeremiah 12:13-14 God promises that when we call on Him, come to Him and pray to Him, He will listen. When we look for Him we will find Him. He will make sure we are not disappointed. Mark Batterson says, "Prayer is the difference between you fighting for God and God fighting for you."

Our friends challenged us to pray more for them and others as they continued to pray for us. I can never tell you how many people came up to us, often times just a tap on the shoulder in passing saying, "Don't forget, we pray for you every day!" That was so very humbling. Sometimes we felt so self-absorbed that it seemed we only prayed for ourselves and our family. I remember the day I cried out to the Lord on the way home from leaving Jack in the hospital. I told the Lord I had all I could do to keep myself together. I couldn't imagine that was where He wanted me because I had nothing left for anyone else. Sometimes I spent a few days pouring my heart out to the Lord and I did dwell on us. In those times I believe I grew to understand God's ways more and in the end have more to help others in their time of need. There is a deep knowing when you experience God's peace and presence for yourself because of personal hurt instead of knowing He provides all in theory.

There is no doubt in my mind that the prayers of our family and friends made a significant difference in our experience. We asked God often to bless those who were blessing us.

Chapter 8

THE SOVEREIGNTY OF GOD

"God gives people the exact experiences he wants them to have in order to shape the specific destiny He's designed for them."
Steven Furtick

Jack had the ability to look at things with a different viewpoint than most of us would. One day I said I felt like lying on the floor and kicking like a spoiled child yelling that this was not the way retirement was supposed to be. He said, "Honey, what good would that do? Either God is sovereign or He isn't." When I was having a self-pity day, I resented his calm, sweet, CONSTANT Christ-like spirit. Most days I deeply appreciated it.

Through the difficult times we learned to see Jesus in His grace, His love and His peace!! After so many years of struggling, we purposely began to claim His love and peace much more quickly than we had before. It's so easy to get shaken when the doctor gives you bad news. We found that if we indulge in feelings of pity and regret it so easily leads to resentment and bad feelings. We consciously started to develop the habit of telling Jesus we trusted Him right away. That was much better than stewing and getting upset before we turn things back to

God. We knew none of it was a surprise to Him. He knew about all this hurt and frustration way before we did. Since we were coming to see Christ in His love, grace and peace, we more easily were able to trust Him. It's very freeing to be able to turn things over to the Lord. When we acknowledge the fact that He is sovereign and that sovereignty is totally covered with love for us, it helps us put life in a different light.

We truly believe that when we are living in obedience, trusting Him, and seeking to honor Him to the best of our ability, the outcome then is up to Him, not us.

Furtick says he doesn't want his life to slip by without seeing God show Himself mightily in his life. This so helped us express our feelings. We wanted God to be seen mightily in what He was doing in us. We asked God to produce a harvest of obedience in our lives, obedience that glorified God. The darker it gets, the brighter our faith can shine. We often noticed that much of the time God doesn't step in until the last moment. That's what makes it faith. Furtick says, "If my problem is too big for me, it's just the right size for God. God wants His power and resources to seep from every pore of my life."

We truly believe that when we are living in obedience, trusting Him and seeking to honor Him to the best of our ability, the outcome then is up to Him, not us.

We learned that our prayers should not always be to 'get us out' of our circumstances. We learned to pray for God to 'get us through.' We found God had reasons far beyond our personal reasons. His answer is rarely the easy way out. His answer is the best and is what brings Him the most glory. After all, the primary purpose of our prayers is not to change our circumstances, but to change us.

One Sunday morning our pastor talked about trials. "Every trial I face is allowed by God for my ultimate good. They are trials, not consequences. Trials are allowed, not caused. Trials need not steal my joy. Trials bring me to the power of God. Trials prove I am God's child. Trials increase my endurance. We only develop endurance by enduring. Trials build intimacy with Jesus. Until I embrace my trial in submission to God, I will not reap the good. I don't understand it all but He does."

Sunday morning was always filled with truths to tuck away in our hearts and apply to our lives.

Chapter 9

Spritzing God's Grace

He giveth more grace when the burden grows greater,
He sendeth more strength when the labors increase:
To added affliction He addeth his mercy,
To multiplied trials His multiplied peace.

When we have exhausted our store of endurance,
When our strength has failed ere the day is half-done,
When we reach the end of our hoarded resources,
Our Father's full giving is only begun.

His love has no limit, His grace has no measure,
His power has no boundary known unto men;
For out of His infinite riches in Jesus
He giveth and giveth and giveth again!

He Giveth More Grace
by Annie Johnson Flint and Hubert Mitchell

We would have told you that we understood God's grace. Certainly the grace of God to have given His Son to die for us is paramount. I don't think, however, that we had seen the magnitude of the grace of God in our daily affairs.

It is His grace that heals our broken hearts. It is His grace that keeps us from falling off the edge when things go wrong. It is His grace that helps us forgive and love when we have been hurt. His grace is offered to each of us for any need.

One Sunday morning, our friend Wes asked Jack how he was able to remain so upbeat in spite of all the difficulties. By this time he was not speaking any more than he had to. He responded simply, "God's grace." Then he was asked if it was true that as things get worse, God pours on more of His grace. Jack responded, "Yes, that is true." When he got to the car he told me about the conversation. He was so excited, he took my hand and said, "Honey, the Lord just showed me something. We don't have to worry, the worse things get; the more God will pour His grace on us. He will do the balancing act! We don't have to worry. He will do the balancing act." It was like God had just given him a new revelation and he was as excited as a kid with a new toy.

Jack needed some dental work done. It was about a three hour procedure. We had to cancel two times because he didn't feel well enough to go. We felt guilty about cancelling something that the doctor had reserved that much time for. Finally we took a time when someone else had cancelled. Jack still had the bad cough and if he couldn't get his hand up to his mouth fast enough, he sprayed all over as he coughed. This cough came and went for over three years. It seemed worse the particular morning we headed for the dentist.

When we parked I asked him what he was going to do when there were three faces staring into his face, his arms under the apron and he had to cough. He very sweetly took my hands and said, "Honey, God poured lots of grace on me this morning and I know it is going to be alright. Let's just trust Him." Only a half hour into the procedure, the dentist came out and said, "This is going so well. We have recently started a new procedure that is working very well. He should be done in about another half hour and it will cost you $500 instead of $1500." I almost burst into tears and wept. It is times like that when I see Jesus looking down and smiling. I'm sure He thinks it was too bad I didn't trust Him to start with. It would have saved all the emotional energy I wasted. Jack came out smiling!!!! On the way home he said he only had one little cough that didn't amount to anything.

> *We don't have to worry, the worse things get; the more God will pour His grace on us.*

When my friend Nancy prayed with me sometime later, she thanked the Lord for spritzing grace on Jack the morning of his dental appointment. I love that word picture. Can't you just see God spritzing grace on you???

I had begun to see that God was pouring an extra measure of His grace on my precious honey. It thrilled me to have him be so encouraged by the Holy Spirit and God's presence. I began to see that Holiness is a by-product of seeing Jesus in His grace. When you experience Jesus and His love and grace every day, your heart is transformed inwardly. This is not outward behavior modification. This is real change that is brought on by a heart touched by God's grace.

Chapter 10

HAVING A HUNGER AND THIRST FOR GOD'S WORD

"The Bible is the only book whose author is always present when one reads it." Author Unknown

Jack had a keen insight into God's Word. There was one simple reason for that, he spent a lot of time there. Even when our sons were growing up, when any one of the four of us got grouchy one of us would say, "How long has it been since you spent time with the Lord?" We have never been able to stay on top of things without that quiet time. I believe God's Word got so indwelt in Jack during those years that it carried him through the years when he couldn't read anymore. Up until the end he quoted Scripture and its reference.

It never ceases to amaze me that even Christians will try to go through life spending little or no time in God's Word. The Bible is God's love letter to us. It is one of His ways of giving us direction, peace and joy. We throw the most powerful, the most satisfying asset of a lifetime out the window. We can't claim His promises if we don't know them. Let me encourage you to ask God to give you a hunger and thirst for His Word. There are not words to describe what studying His Word will do for you.

One day Jack said, "Each week I get slower and do less, but it just causes me to trust Him more." He said he often had to remind himself of Ps. 46:1 "God is my refuge and strength, an ever present help in trouble." We really believe that if God would pull back the curtain of life and allow us to see Heavenly realms; we would understand all we are going through right now. However, He has designed us to live by faith not by sight. II Cor. 5:7

My journal says, I often felt weak and discouraged. I found that when I was in that spot, I would react to circumstances emotionally. That always got me into trouble; it only makes bad situations worse. God would refresh me as I got into His Word. Time is one of the most important things we can give God. It tells Him that He is important to us and that we can't make it without Him. Other times I could tell God was changing me. I saw that either God would change the situation or change my heart. Many times, He changed my heart. He changed my priorities, my purpose, and my point of contentment. I said, "He is giving me what I need, not what I thought I wanted." God always provides a way.

II Corinthians 4:16-18 "We do not lose heart, but though our outer man is decaying, yet our inner man is being renewed day by day. For momentary, light affliction is producing for us an eternal weight of glory far beyond all comparison, while we look not at the things which are seen; for the things which are seen are temporal, but the things which are not seen are eternal." NASB

There is no promise in Scripture that Christ followers will escape all suffering. There is a promise that He will be there during the ordeal. That surely was the case for us. We do God a dishonor when every time we suffer; we think He has dropped the reins. His ways are sometimes different than our ways, but they are His ways. Our duty is to trust that He is a faithful Creator who only has our best interests at heart. Jack entrusted himself, for the long haul, to a faithful Creator. It made all the difference in the way he lived out his suffering and ultimately died in Christ.

I am convinced that when we give Him more of ourselves, He gives us more of Himself!

I am convinced that when we give Him more of ourselves, He gives us more of Himself!

Chapter 11

The Enemy, Satan!!

"Our imagination of the future, which is almost always dictated by fear of some kind, rarely, if ever, pictures God there with us." William P. Young

A couple times we called and asked our pastor to come and pray with us. It seemed discouragement was coming from every angle. Sometimes it took us longer to recognize it was the enemy. Jack was very conscious of the enemy in his life. At the same time, he often reminded us in Bible study that too much of the time we bring our own problems on and then falsely give Satan the credit. Pastor Rick reminded us that worship music will help fight the enemy. We found ourselves either listening to sacred music or TBN (Trinity Broadcasting Network) most of the time. Even in the last year when Jack slept through much of what he was listening to, he loved hearing pastors in the background preaching God's Word. The air in our home was filled with music or words honoring God. It seemed to help make our home a habitat for the Holy Spirit's presence.

A month or so before Jack died, I asked what he wanted me to say when people asked how to pray for him. He said, "Pray that the enemy would not steal my peace." You would be surprised at the lies Satan tells me. It angered me that the enemy never gives up. He will attack us until the end. I asked Jack what he did when the enemy told him lies. He said, "I just keep quoting Scripture and reminding the enemy I am covered with the blood of Jesus." The enemy seeks to devour our faith. God seeks to refine it.

CHAPTER 12

THE PEACE THAT GOES BEYOND ALL UNDERSTANDING

"He is no fool who gives up what he cannot keep to gain what he cannot lose." Jim Elliot

"You will guard me and keep me in perfect and constant peace as my mind (both its inclination and its character) is stayed on You, because I commit myself to You, lean on You, and hope confidently in You." Isaiah 26:3 (AMP)

Philippians 4:7 (AMP) "God's peace (shall be mine, that tranquil state of a soul assured of its salvation through Christ, and so fearing nothing from God and being content with its earthly lot of whatever sort that is, that peace) which transcends all understanding shall garrison and mount guard over my heart and mind in Christ Jesus."

Jack was puzzled about having a restless day. I asked him if he didn't think it was just anxiousness over everything. He so sweetly said, "Everything, what would I have to be anxious about?" I suggested maybe dying, the process, just how will it happen, etc. He said, "Oh no, honey, I'm not afraid of dying. Why would I worry about that, Jesus is on my side." I wept those same tears of joy and sadness. He asked why I was crying because it was the truth. Who talks that way unless you have an extra measure of God's grace and I told Jack that I felt that way. He nodded his head, yes.

God has used Jack's peace to encourage and comfort my heart. I truly believe that God's grace is there for us when we need it, as we need it and in the measure that we need it. We need not live our lives with anxiousness or fear. God never misses a beat. When we need His grace, He knows the need better than we do and He will pour the grace on. As we live in difficult days economically and politically, we can be confident that God's grace will be enough for each day's need. I know that not only from God's Word but because I have experienced it.

Why would I be afraid of dying . . . Jesus is on my side.

I feel the Holy Spirit beautifully led Jack through his suffering. Our pastor said at the memorial service, "I believe Jack died well because He lived well." One of Jack's desires was that others would also allow the Holy Spirit to bless them with God's grace and peace. He had a heart for others struggling with hurt and not turning to the Lord for strength and peace.

There was a time that he thought he should be dying sooner and it should be easier. He was frustrated that he was still here. One night he had me awakened to talk. He took my hands and said, "Honey, is this the day I go home?" We talked some about how we just don't know but God knows. I reassured him that God knew just how long Jack's life would be and just when He would bring him home.

One morning he was especially feeing like it was taking too long. In his frustration he reached for the trapeze bar over his bed. He held real tight looking up to heaven and began singing "My Jesus, I love Thee." We sang two verses together. You might remember that the last line of that hymn is "If ever I need Thee, my Jesus, 'tis now." We sang some other hymns and he returned to "My Jesus, I love Thee" again then settled down to sleep. I have wondered if in his spirit he didn't see Jesus and all he could do was respond with "My Jesus, I love Thee."

Some have said that even in his silence, there was a peace about him that permeated the room.

I was so blessed to have a husband who chose peace through those years of trials. Even though I seemed to have to work harder on myself to reach peace, I did live in peace most of the time. After a while I found it so much easier to live in peace than to live in worry and anxiety. There are not words to describe the difference of totally giving your life to the Lord and knowing that He is in charge and not you. Without the process, there is no progress.

One day another one of our Hospice nurses called. She asked how I was. I told her, "I often cry and it was a very sad time, but I do have peace." She just responded with, "Really?" I told her that I'd better have peace or that I needed to shut my mouth. Jack and I are always claiming that God loves us and He knows best. We are often saying that He only allows what is best for us and that we trust Him. Either I too experience that peace that comes from God or I need to shut my mouth. As I was talking I realized I was a bit worked up and coming on strong. I'm sure the Holy Spirit was my inspiration. It was a powerful surge of excitement that shot through my body. It was as though the Lord said, "You're right. I have proven myself faithful through the worst of times. Now you will tell people of my faithfulness and how they too can trust Me. You can say it with even more conviction since you have experienced it." I believe God used Laura that day to help me put into words what He was showing me.

Chapter 13

There Is No Doubt That God Could Have Healed Jack

*"If God chooses to heal me, I trust Him.
If He chooses not to heal me, I trust Him.
My greatest joy comes from resting in Him."* Jackson Herr

There is no doubt in our minds that God could have healed my dear Jack. When things first started we believed with all our hearts that he would be healed. Many people prayed over Jack. We were always encouraged. After an extended period of time God seemed to tell us that He wanted us to just rest in Him, not continually strive for physical healing but to live to bring Him glory no matter what the outcome. There came a time when Jack said, "If God heals me I trust Him, if He chooses not to heal me I trust Him. My greatest joy comes from just resting in Him."

We often asked God to touch and heal Jack. It just wasn't our overwhelming obsession. We also see resting as being active, not passive. I am reminded of what Jesus said on the cross: "My Father, if it is possible, let this cup of suffering be taken away from me. Yet, I want your will to be done, not mine." Matthew 26:39.

Jesus shows us what to do when God doesn't give us what we want.

"And this small and temporary trouble I suffer will bring me a tremendous and eternal glory, much greater than the trouble. For I fix my attention, not on things that are seen, but on things that are unseen. What can be seen lasts only for a time, but what cannot be seen lasts forever." II Corinthians 4:17-18 (GNT). We began to see that even things that seemed so disappointing and hurtful had eternal value.

We believe that sometimes we see a miracle of healing in someone. Other times we see that person become the miracle of grace. I personally believe God greatly uses those who for some reason are not healed here on earth when they stay faithful and exhibit the miracle of grace in their lives. Either way, God is a miracle working God. I believe Jack's sweet spirit and total trust is the way God chose to use Jack in the last years of his life. This was a new ministry that God had chosen for Jack. In some respects, God used Jack in an even greater way the last few years of his life than the many before.

Sometimes we see a miracle of healing, sometimes a miracle of grace. Either way, God is a miracle working God.

Joyce Meyer says, "Miracles don't grow us up. Only when we have to walk through a situation, depending wholly on God, do we grow in Him."

Chapter 14

Dream, Struggle, Prize

"Our uniqueness is God's gift to us, but it's also our gift back to God." Mark Batterson

"No matter what our dream is in life, whether it be material, physical or spiritual, there will always be a struggle before we reach our goal." Jackson Herr

One night Jack seemed very weak, quiet and not himself. I asked him if he was discouraged. He said, "No." I asked how he could not be discouraged. He gently said, "It's just the struggle." I was a bit confused and asked if he could explain. (Because of Jack's brain surgery, his speech was not real clear. He also had lots of saliva so he didn't talk much. He used short sentences.)

He said, "Remember in life there is always the dream or goal, however we have to go through the struggle before we finally have the prize or reward." I asked him if that was a spiritual principle we had used as a business principle or a business principle he turned into a spiritual principle. He said, "Both, I got it from my friend Jerry Webb and I have never forgotten it."

To bring honor and glory to the Lord is the goal; however, it often seems we grow the most through the times of struggle. In Ephesians 3: 20-21 it says, "God can do anything, you know—far more than you could ever imagine or guess or request in your wildest dreams! He does it not by pushing us around but by working within us, his Spirit deeply and gently within us." (The Message) Often God uses time as a trainer to teach us to wait on Him. It seems the more extreme the situation, the more likely we are to see His power and glory at work. In *Jesus Calling*, it is suggested that we need to view our difficulties as setting the scene for His glorious intervention. God rarely reveals His grand design, he reveals Himself. God loves us just the way we are, but He loves us too much to leave us the way we are.

Jack and I both see our purpose in life is to bring honor and glory to God. We live to hear God say, "Well done, good and faithful servant."

Whatever struggle God allows us to go through will be worth the prize of hearing "Well done."

Chapter 15

I Choose Grandpa

Our grandchildren have been one of the biggest blessings to our hurting hearts during these last years.

One Christmas Eve during our devotional time, we somehow were discussing the importance of encouraging each other. Nicole, our daughter-in-law, suggested we each take one person and tell them why they are special to us. Immediately our grandson Dakotah, who was 9 at the time, raised his hand and yelled, "I take Grandpa." So sweetly he said, "Grandpa is good at turning people to Jesus without saying a word. It's because of his good attitude."

That takes no explanation.

CHAPTER 16

FAITHFUL FAMILY AND FRIENDS ARE A GIFT!!

"Stay connected with believers! To connect is to bind or fasten together for a common purpose. Relationships that promote Christ-like living are necessary as well as an act of obedience. We need to be accountable to others....Don't expect perfection from anyone; instead praise a willing and obedient heart. Whisper sweet words to your family unit. The family represents God's choicest relationships."
Cheryl Matson/Brown

Our sons and daughters-in-law were faithful. The years took a toll on them as well. We are so thankful for their love and support. Our grandchildren were like balm to our hearts.

Dakotah's love and tenderness toward his grandpa meant more than words can express. Garrett's fun, upbeat, light spirit helped to lift the air. Madalyn was born December 6, 2013. Grandpa got to hold her shortly after she was born. At that time and until he died, her smile and content spirit blessed him as he had her by his side. As we have prayed for Dakotah and Garrett, Jack began praying for Madalyn's future spouse when she was two weeks old. We had planned to celebrate our 50th

anniversary on August 14, 2014. In February a number of friends suggested we might want to celebrate early to be sure Jack would be here. Our kids graciously agreed. They took it on and in one month pulled together a beautiful celebration of our lives. We were blessed beyond words as family and friends came to honor us. Our hearts were full and overflowing. Jack said it was so wonderful that he thought everyone should have a party like that before they die. The following day cousins and friends who had come from out of town came to our house to spend more time with us. As I stood and watched them one by one go to the bedroom to spend their last time with Jack here on earth, the Lord seemed to point out how beautifully it was coming together for them to say good bye to my honey. He reminded me of how He found such joy in blessing us. It thrilled my heart to see God at work fulfilling His beautiful plan.

My sister Cherrie never wearied in listening to us and was so faithful. A couple weeks before Jack died, knowing she would not be able to answer her phone, he had me call my niece Melanie so he could hear her voice on her answering machine. He left her a message that none of us could understand but it was filled with love for her.

One of the many blessings we had was a group of friends who decided they would come to spend the night with Jack so I could sleep. A dear friend and gifted organizer, Joyce, set up a schedule. Friends came two to three nights a week for many months. What a blessing they were to both of us. I remember sitting in the living room waiting for them to come through the door at 10:00 p.m. The last two to three weeks they were here every night.

One night Jack asked our friend and caregiver, Barb, if she realized he was dead and on his way to heaven. She explained that he wasn't dead but God was preparing him. They had a good talk. We wondered later if in the spirit he saw her as he looked down.

Our friends sang, read God's Word, prayed, told stories, listened to his stories, gave back rubs, fluffed pillows, and just simply loved Jack. They were the church of God at work. God bless them.

Just knowing they cared and loved us enough to give of their time and energy blessed us beyond words. They were a gift from God.

Chapter 17

We Each Show Our Love in Different Ways

Brother, sister, let me serve you,
Let me be as Christ to you;
Pray that I may have the grace to
let you be my servant too.

We are pilgrims on a journey;
We're together on this road.
We are here to help each other
walk the mile and bear the load.

I will weep when you are weeping;
When you laugh, I'll laugh with you.
I will share your joy and sorrow
till we've seen this journey thro'.

When we sing to God in heaven,
We shall find such harmony.
Born of all we've known together
of Christ's love and agony.

The Servant Song by Richard Gillard

It always amazed me how many ways people came up with to show us that they cared and loved us. One special message from Marcia back at the beginning said, "I knew you would be gone. I just wanted to remind you that we love you and are praying for you. You don't have to call back." Nancy would send a text saying, "You have been on my mind all day. Is there something special I should be praying about?" Friends would come up to me in church, just give me a little squeeze and say, "We need a new email so we know what to be praying for." Friends would make and send cards over and over. Many would say, "I'm not just praying for Jack, I'm praying for you too. How are YOU?" Sometimes people would bring food. Sometimes people would offer to stay with Jack for a couple hours so I could get out.

I think I can honestly say we went to church on Sunday morning not only to worship and hear a wonderful message but also to be loved. I can't stress enough how much love means when everything else seemingly is not good. We have often said that the church did what the church is supposed to do as far as we were concerned. They definitely reached out to us with love.

One of the last few weekends before Jack died the kids were all here. Our daughters-in-law went in to spend extended time with Jack. Nicole, who is a very tender-hearted nurse, put lotion on Jack's body. She gave him a beautiful massage. She was always so tender with him. Alison was there often fluffing and moving pillows, doing her best to make him comfortable. He loved it and it blessed my heart seeing how they ministered in their ways to his needs. It was such a reminder that God has gifted each of us differently and when we each do our part, hearts are blessed.

Chapter 18

Our Life Is a Tapestry!

My life is but a weaving between my God and me.
I cannot choose the color He weaveth steadily.

Oft 'times He weaveth sorrow; and I in foolish pride,
Forget He sees the upper and I the underside.

Not 'til the loom is silent and the shuttles cease to fly,
Will God unroll the canvas and reveal the reason why.

The dark threads are as needful in the
weaver's skillful hand
As the threads of gold and silver in the pattern
He has planned.

He knows, He loves, He cares; nothing
this truth can dim.
He gives the very best to those who
leave the choice to Him.

The Tapestry by Corrie Ten Boom

One day, as much as I loved my dear husband, I too was having a heavy heart over Jack still suffering and not being in heaven yet. When one of our Hospice nurses, Lucy Dunn, came to the door, I asked her if she could give us a little idea of how much longer this would take. She so beautifully said, "Our life is like a tapestry. The top is beautiful. The underside is very unattractive. We are only seeing the messy underside of

Remember we aren't writing this story, God is!

Jack's life right now. We just don't understand. God sees the top. He sees the beautiful total picture. He knows what has to happen here on the underside to make things complete on the top. When it is complete, He will take Jack home. When she walked out the door, she stopped and looked back and said, "Remember, we aren't writing this story, God is!"

What a blessing!!!!!

Chapter 19

Leaving This World and Going Home

"Precious in the sight of the Lord is the death of His godly ones." Psalms 116:15 ASB

As Jack was dying, even though I didn't realize it at that time, I was singing to him.

In His time, In His time, He makes all things beautiful in His time, Lord please show me every day

As You're teaching me Your way, That You do just what You say, In Your time.

In Your time, In Your time, You make all things beautiful in Your time.

Lord, my life to You I bring, May each song I have to sing Be to You a lovely thing,

In Your time.

I raised my hand to the Lord and told Him that this was not just another song. We meant this. He knew we had trusted Him for years even though often times we didn't understand. I told Him we still trusted Him to take my honey home in His perfect time and He would make it beautiful. Jack squeezed my hand with energy and took his last breath.

It was as though Jack agreed with what I had just sung and spoken to the Lord. It was a blessed moment as we concluded our nearly 50 years together with our dear Heavenly Father. I thanked the Lord and Jack many times over for the perfect blessing of pulling our lives together in one final beautiful package. The intimacy Jack and I had with Jesus at that moment I wouldn't trade for anything in the world. It was an honor to be with the love of my life when he so peacefully took his last breath. It was like I could almost feel his spirit leave his body. It was such a significant reminder that once the spirit is gone we are merely a shell. I could see him entering the glory of heaven. God's purpose for Jack's life had been accomplished and it was time to take him home.

He makes all things beautiful in His time.

As soon as I told our son Matt he said, "Dad is walking!!" Our son Jeff and his wife Nicole were on their way here when I called to tell them that Jack was with Jesus. They had sensed it was the end and had decided to try to be here when he died. Jeff immediately began apologizing for not being here. I quickly said he had nothing to feel bad about. They had been here plenty in the past months. His dad and I may not have had the beautiful intimate time with Jesus if the family had been here. Again, God knew better. I cried tears of joy and sadness

God doesn't stand aloof as we die watching us agonize. He comes to us in His spirit and sustains us.

all at the same time. I held my sweetheart and gave him to Jesus. I thanked God for giving him to me for 50 years. God, again, proved Himself to be faithful at that very moment. God doesn't stand aloof as we die watching us agonize. He comes to us in His spirit and sustains us. His spirit helped Jack die as strong as He helped him live. Courage that we never thought was possible was ours through Christ.

God is the Composer. Your life is His musical score.
God is the Artist. Your life is His canvas.
God is the Architect. Your life is His blueprint.
God is the Writer. You are His book.
Mark Batterson

CHAPTER 20

I AM CLAIMING MY PEACE AND JOY

Because Jack knew Jesus Christ as his Lord and Savior, we know Jack's life did not cease the day he died. His spirit is alive and well today. The minute Jack's physical life was taken away, his eternal life was beginning. If we believe God created his life, then we must be willing to release it back to Him for His care, calling and keeping.

Our family has had such sweet times together both before Jack died and still after his death. I see God working in each of us, changing us, in one way or another. Seeing change in hearts thrills me because that is precisely what all these heartaches, pain and trials are for . . . to change us.

Since then I've thanked God for the difficult things He helped me work through with Jack at my side. There were times I had resented all my responsibilities. Jack was a good teacher and helped me think things through. It wasn't until after he died that I realized how much he had helped me. God thought of everything.

I know God will make a new way for me. Like a jigsaw puzzle, God causes everything to work together for our good. I have no doubt that He will bless and take care of me. I have learned to trust Him. The way may have seemed long at times, taken a few years, I may have fussed and squirmed, but I have learned to totally trust my Savior. My dear husband learned to totally trust and I have chosen to do the same. It is very freeing to put your life in His hands and leave the results up to Him.

I want to encourage you to take every opportunity to cherish and express love and appreciation to your loved one. Jack was the love of my life. We had a close relationship. He was my very best friend. To us, one of the facets of love was being able to depend on each other. If it is possible, I would have been one who told him too many times how deeply I loved him. We covered every issue we could think of as far as any hurts left, any bad feelings, anything that would linger later. As much as I loved him he knew I had released him to Jesus. He knew I would be alright when he went Home.

> *Because Jack knew Jesus Christ as his Lord and Savior, we know Jack's life did not cease the day he died. His spirit is alive and well today.*

IN SUMMARY

I believe the lives we lived in the last ten to fifteen years were not God's second best for us. I believe they were His best. He knew what was going on in our lives and He knew why. I learned to trust Him then; I choose to trust Him now.

Made in the USA
San Bernardino, CA
14 August 2016